# 10
# STRATEGIES TO DEFEAT
# STRESS AND DEPRESSION

*Creating an Internal Safeguard
against Stress and Depression*

## CHARLES MWEWA

Published by:

AFRICA IN CANADA PRESS (ACP)
Ottawa, Ontario
Canada
www.acpress.ca

Republished edition.

ISBN-13: 978-1-988251-46-2

For

*Bwalya*

R.I.P.

# Contents

# Introduction

Stress is defined as the feeling of being overwhelmed or unable to cope with mental or emotional pressure.[1]

Depression is from the word "depress" or a sense of feeling extremely low or compressed. In medical terms, there are common depressions and what is known as a major depressive disorder.[2]

Depression or major depressive disorder is a common and serious medical illness that negatively affects how you feel, the way you think and how you act. It has been wildly agreed that both stress and depression exhibit the following symptoms: Sadness, loss of interest in activities one usually enjoys, uncontrollable mood swings, decreased energy and fatigue.

Some of these symptoms can become physical, such as exhaustion,

---

[1] https://www.mentalhealth.org.uk › a-to-z › stress (accessed: June 21, 2021)
[2] https://www.psychiatry.org/patients-families/depression/what-is-depression

loss of appetite, trouble sleeping at night or even being unable to concentrate on task or a feeling of inadequacy – leading to slowed movements, difficulty thinking and death of both the mind and the body. Stressed and depressed people may more usually than not contemplate suicides and may lose interest in sex or romance. Depressed individuals may also feel that God doesn't love them or that He loves others more than He loves them. Stress and depression can be dealt with using simple habits proposed in this book.

# 1 UNIVERSAL SOOTHER

Start your day with a prayer or meditation. This is a universal soother, and it doesn't matter whether you are religious or irreligious. Prayer or meditation looks inside of you, and not outside.

When the internal faculties are at peace, energy is transferred to all the parts of you. You gain strength and wisdom to handle all that life might throw at you. It is advisable to do this first thing in the morning before your mind and heart are corrupted by the worries and troubles of the day ahead.

Perfect meditation unites the mind, body and spirit, and it creates a neutral platform where humanity and nature coalesce. Prayer, meditation and yoga are some of the universally acclaimed methods of achieving ascendancy.

Some of the depressive moods are like clots in the system. They prevent the smooth flow of peace, good thoughts and benevolent ideas. They cloud one's memories and feelings of wholeness. They are internally-imbedded. Prayer or meditation moves them out of the way so that good thoughts and wellness can flow freely.

To cultivate a genuine meditative habit, do the following:

- Belong to a religion or faith group or join a clean yoga class;
- Select empowering verses from its sacred book or recite the meditation routine, regularly, especially early in the morning. If you are a Christian, pray every morning, setting aside time to reflect on Scriptures and the goodness of the Lord.
- Confess victory, favor, success, love, acceptance or whatever is good, noble, praiseworthy, and etc., into your own life.
- Believe and live it.

## 2  MESSAGING MATTERS

Do not start your day with external messaging: Indeed, you heard right, emails, texts, mails, and all forms of external messaging affect your energy and wit levels in the morning.

Unless you are very sure what message you will find, put away opening your message until you have dealt with your priorities for the day. News, especially, bad news, can spoil your entire day. The good news is that you have the power to control what you hear.

And the same goes for TV, social media and so on. If you are not expecting good news, don't access your messages. Do something more empowering first and then, at some appropriate time, access your messages. If you are expecting a particularly bad message or news, plan on how to receive it and process it. A bad message or news is like a sharp sword piercing your soul, mind and heart. You wouldn't allow such a weapon to reach your naked skin, so do the same; protect your heart. Anything you access first, if it is bad news, may set your day's agenda and may lead to increased stress or depression, if not managed well.

Be deliberate, inject yourself with good things, such as, encouraging messages, uplifting songs, edifying TV channels and helpful social media platforms. Stop poisoning your mind and soul with stress-laden content and depressive messages.

# 3  START TO FINISH

Finish what you start. Yes, if you have a habit of not finishing what you started, you may be deliberately increasing your stress levels.

Unfinished work unsettles your heart and mind. It is like there is always something you have forgotten, and that feeling may unsettle you throughout the day. When you start something, be sure to finish it. And this also leads to success.

The most effective people on earth are also people who complete what they started. Most procrastinators don't achieve nearly as much as non-procrastinators. Unfinished projects may lead to depressive moods or episodes.

Care must be taken that one is not dully obsessed with finishing their project leading to stress or depression. To avoid this, the following steps may be taken:

1.  Define your project – what is

it that you want to achieve or complete? And why do you want to achieve it, is it for profit, pleasure, legacy or others?

2. Plan your project – how, where and when you will begin and end? This enables you to be focused and to prioritize your time, resources and energy.

3. Have a plan within the plan or call it Plan B – this is particularly important if you are going to avert depression and stress. One of the reasons why people are depressed is because they fail to complete what they started, and if they have started already, they may still be depressed if their project fails. To curb this, always have a plan within a plan, so that if the major plan fails, you can continue to work with Plan B. Plan A should have

generated resources or means to quickly jump into Plan B. This way, you will always have something to live for, the reason not to give up or die early.

A good plan is a buffer for the mind and heart. Even if it delays to be fulfilled (probably owing to lack of resources), the mind will be at peace. This attitude should be had even in doing day-to-day mundane things.

It doesn't matter what your station in life is, you will always have something to do – if you are a housewife, you have home chores to run, just make sure that you complete them thoroughly and excellently. If you are a breadwinner, make sure you do your work, thoroughly and excellently. If you are a student, ensure that you complete your assignments before or by the due date, and if you are preparing for examinations, do so thoroughly and excellently.

People who take interest in completing what they have started are, on average, more satisfied than those who start and do not finish.

# 4 MONEY OR HONEY

**M**anage your money well. In fact, money can be both a distresser and a distress. It can be both the disease and the antidot. It can be both the problem and the remedy.    Money causes so much stress and is a source of depression for more people than we may know. The ability to manage money well can relieve stress and bring great relief and joy. There is stress if you don't have it. There is tension if you have it. And there is depression if you lose it.

You have heard of this mantra: Now these three remain, love, hope and faith, and the greatest is love. They are all great, thank heaven. So, if you don't have money, hope. When you have it, love. And if you lose it, have faith. And when you have it, the best way to manage money is to GIVE IT or USE IT or INVEST IT.

The issue of money causes stress even to beloved couples, couples who have everything going well for them. It shouldn't come as shock that money and the way it is handled is one of the reasons why some marriages fail and couples split-up or divorce. But it can be handled, and this calls for good management of money. No-one is an expert in money handling, even the money manager herself needs to constantly learn how to handle money.

It is for this reason that the issue of money should be given due priority. Money can be as bitter as wormwood or as sweet as honey, depending on how it is managed. The security of having money or wealth can go a long way to relieving stress and preventing depression.

# 5 THOUGHT PURGER

Purge negative thoughts, ignore persisting ones. Have you ever gone to bed and spent the best part of it being bombarded by negative or bad thoughts?

Somehow, all your bad thoughts gang up on you and begin to, literally, beat you up. All that didn't go well during the day and all that was embarrassing, humiliating, frustrating or demeaning now find a way to you. You try to resist, to no avail.

Sometimes, even the old negative experiences, failures, defeats, shames and disappointments may show up. The end point is to get you overwhelmed with all kinds of low-moods, fear, worry, anxiety and, of course, stress. Somehow you now remember that you were abused, rejected, insulted or worse. Then you find yourself folding off like a beaten puppy.

And yet, you are the one thinking. Thinking is only helpful if you are thinking something that is good, praiseworthy, building, noble, or similarly-situated thoughts. Any negative thought, any bad thinking robs you of peace and sometimes, may be toxic to your soul.

# 6 MIND GUARD

Deliberately vanquish all bad thoughts from your mind. This takes practice; to learn how to drill off negative thoughts do the following: (1) Decide – decisiveness is an integral part of any recovery regime. Even good medicine may be of no value if it is not taken; (2) Acknowledge all the bad thoughts, then ignore them. Because you cannot manage that which you haven't acknowledged or recognized. Bad thoughts are painful, and sometimes, they can weigh you down; (3) Do something or watch something or read something or listen to something or say something nice, building or lovely. This is only necessary in the interim as you work on a routine. Once you become used to this routine, clearing bad thoughts will happen with less effort.

Repeat the three steps until you conquer the bad thoughts, fall asleep or attain to the goal you desire. If you continue to do the above day-after-day, you will reach a stage where you will begin to block bad thoughts at will.

Bad thoughts, worry, anxiety or depressive mental naggings bring negative energy which filter throughout the human system and may cause all kinds of undesirables, such as low mood, depression, stress, weakness, lack of confidence, self-pity or even death. It is unwise to keep on entertaining bad thoughts; they are lethal and dangerous.

Stop them.

Our minds are linked to our physical environment. Memory is jogged-up when you come across distressing or depressing objects and events. Avoid anything that reminds you of a bad past or of an event that led you to being stressed or depressed in the first place. Burn, destroy, incinerate, delete, dump or shred anything that dispirits you. In this regard, out of sight may mean out of mind.

# 7 RECORD OF WRONGS

Don't keep a record of wrongs. We have all done something we may not be proud of. In religious terms, we have sinned. Legally, we may have been wrong or guilty or liable for something. Morally, we might have done something that was not right. And socially, we might have offended someone.

It is true that all of us in our lifetime we will wrong, offend and disappoint many. We might even have betrayed those who loved, cherished and supported us. All these may bring tremendous contrition and sorrow upon us. It is already overwhelming that we did all that, why make it even worse by reliving such traumatic moments?

Indeed, we become depressed each time we dwell on our not-so-good past. We must confront our past if we are going to enjoy the present and tame the future. However, we must remember the past only in as far as we need to acknowledge the problem before we can find a solution.

Shelving under or attempting to ignore an obvious flaw is not good, either. So, we must face up to our bad past, and even confront our deep-seated disappointments and embarrassments. But we should not allow them to overwhelm us and rule over us. However outstandingly egregious the disappointment, embarrassment or humiliation was, it did not kill us.

In the least, it derailed us, but it never conquered us. We are stressed or depressed because we dwell on our strenuous experiences; we feed them. When they are fed and satisfied they attack us. We ought to be starving our bad experiences so that they can die. When we are wronged or if we wronged others, we need to forgive.

Forgiveness will release us from our distresser; it will liberate us into true freedom. Forgiveness here should not be embroidered into religious connotations; forgiveness is necessary everywhere humans shall gather. Because when humans gather, they are bound to offend one another. Forgiveness first restores wholeness in the forgiver and then it liberates the forgiven. Deep inside of us, we have the power to be free. We have an intrinsic fortress to withstand all manners of depressive attacks.

We ought to allow our inner self to do its work. We ought to release all those who have done us wrong, and in doing so, we are freeing ourselves from our depressors. Some experiences are worse than death, one may say. Experiences such as rape or sexual abuse or assault may be too hard to break. But remember that if you bottle-up your feelings, you will be experiencing the uncomfortable event all over again. You cannot ignore it, either.

The best approach is to acknowledge how bad it was, and then to decide to move on in spite of it. Your abuser may be given another opportunity to torment you if you dwell on the event. Bad or negative experiences and encounters are notorious for repeating themselves through their victims' minds. Your mind should be trained only to retain good, empowering thoughts. This must be done with deliberation. It doesn't happen automatically or accidentally. It takes willpower, effort and self-discipline to remember something. Likewise, it takes an equal amount of effort to forget something awful, traumatic or less empowering.

# 8 TAMING SHAME

Embrace the power of shame, question the benefits of fame. At the root of every depressed or stressed soul, is the feeling of shame. Shame is brought about by consciousness of wrong. It may also be as a result of foolish behavior.

A deep feeling of humiliation hovers around the victim. In their own world, this looks like everything has crumbled. The victim becomes suspicious of every person they meet. This feeling may lead one to isolation and even to the entertainment of suicidal ideations.

Shame is not always bad. To feel ashamed may be a sign that one is a living being with a living conscience. It is more dangerous not to feel shame for acts that are not regarded as ideal than to be ashamed of such acts or behavior. Shame is a referee, an umpire which shows us that we are still part of the collective human race. It reminds us that our actions, attitudes and words have value and can be weapons against good order.

Shame can also be a good teacher. Because when we feel shame, we begin to get better. We begin to adjust our behavior and acts so that we may be a part of our society. When society comes at us and shames us, society is also reacting to its internally accepted norms. There is a balancing act, we feel revulsed by what we did or said and society reacts to eliminate that bad behavior. In this way, the idea of normalcy is restored.

Shame is always with us, except it is powerless if it has not been exposed. Shame is extremely shy. It hates publicity. And that is why a person can live with bad behavior for years until it has been exposed. Even if that person knew that what they did or said in private were wrong, they would have no motivation to stop it until it has been exposed.

Therefore, shame is good for both the individual and society. Without it, renovation, restitution and rehabilitation would be fruitless exercises. When a person is ashamed of their acts, deeds or words, it begins a process to wellness, a process that makes that person relatively better than those whose bad behavior has not been exposed yet.

Shame by itself is neither good nor bad. It is what a person who is ashamed does with shame that matters. To most people, denial is the natural reaction they have to shame. Others do try to hide. While some accept it and then kill themselves. So, it depends on an individual. However, like pain, shame does not last forever. In fact, it is good that the feelings of shame linger for a while. The perceived result would be that such an individual has a rare opportunity to change and better their lives.

The best way to react to shame is to genuinely acknowledge it – privately or publicly – and then institute measures that will allow one to adjust or change their behavior. It may be useful to "disappear" momentarily from the environment that induced shame and seek solace in one's own family or with sympathetic friends. If there are no families or friends to rely upon, one can genuinely and unashamedly dig deeper into their own soul and there find solace.

Some measures to take may include:

- Sharing one's deepest thoughts with a trusted person or professional.

- Taking time off in order to seek recovery from the pain of shame.

- Revising or amending behavior, especially the behavior that led to the shameful event in the first place.

- Accepting or acknowledging the source or cause of the shameful event and seeking better ways to handle or manage it.

- Learning a lesson from the event and be better. Some people have used what shamed them most to create interests and organizations that have gone to helping those in similar situations.

- Laughing at the shameful event. This might sound foolish at first, but a person who has been shamed for an event may not repeat that behavior. And since all humans harbor some secrets which are not yet shamed because they have not been exposed, a person who has been exposed is better than those who haven't been exposed.

- Keeping no records of wrongs.[3]

Taming shame is a necessary part of the recovery process. Shame is one of the underlining factors why people feel low, depressed, stressed or even entertaining ideas of suicide. The above-discussed measures can go a long way in managing shame.

---

[3] See the discussion in Chapter 7

# 9 DIVERSIFIED PARTICULARITY

Think in diversity, not in particularity. Most people who become low and even commit suicide, felt that there was no option left. They were squeezed into the bare minimum and they did not see a way out.

First, they should know that the choice or the state of being lowly or committing suicide is an option they had available.

Second, they should extend that thinking to, "If suicide is an option, then, there may be other options."

And third, there are other available options out there. All that one needs to do is to look for them. A little bit of research may yield glorious results.

No-one experiences stress or depression for no apparent reason. Stress and depression are always linked to some event, occurrence or experience.

And you are stressed or depressed because that particular

event seems to have left you with no chance to complete a goal, fulfill a purpose or be in the state of wellness you anticipated. A stressful or depressing event always tries to convince you that you are finished, that you have no other options. And some people endure depressive and stressing events or even relationships because they, erroneously, believed that they had nowhere else to go or to be. That is a lie. There are always options.

Some people have found their real calling or purpose because they were disappointed with the fake peace or temporary security they had. One person may feel or think that their current job is the most ideal until they are fired. When they lose that job, they may be depressed and have feelings of lowliness. However, they may not know that there is a new, better job waiting for them. The same may be true for divorce or marital breakdown or failure in an examination.

Step it up; you have options.

# 10 EXPIRED EXPERIENCE

U nderstand that you are more than the sum of all your experiences. Experience is defined by practical contact and present observation. Some events that may give rise to painful, shameful and even humiliating experiences have happened in us, to us, or outside of us. In a way, they have become a part of us – our history will not be written without mentioning them. So, it is no longer a matter of what, it is one of how.

The best way to deal with bad experiences is to follow a six-phase-regime (scheme):

1.  Acknowledge the negative or bad experience. It happened to you and to nobody else. It is real and it is part of you. If you have to conquer it, this phase is very important.

2.  Study its nature – what is it, how does it manifest, what are

its devastative impact? If you can't answer those questions, you will never be able to tame it. It will always rule over you.

3. Decide that it shall not rule over you. Decisiveness is very crucial. Some people exacerbate their own negative experiences because of indecisiveness. They entertain it like a developing cancer cell. They dwell on it with repugnance but then they do nothing about it. Or they curdle it like raising a young cobra. When it grows bigger, it will bite.

4. Find a mental routine to fall on. This stage is explained by the contents of Chapter 6.

5. Find others with similar experiences and mentor them.

6. Live with the experience as a badge of honor or love the outcome but hate the

experience. This is especially very important for those who have become pregnant as a result of a rape event. Surely, the rape is a revulsion, a distasteful experience, but if an innocent child was made, take pride in carrying the pregnancy to term and loving the child born. But do not love or entertain the rape experience itself.

The six-phase-scheme can manage any negative experience imaginable. Even for those situations in which you have been ashamed, humiliated, disappointed, abused, neglected or rejected. The six phases can help you to reclaim your power. It can put you back in a place where you would have always wanted to be, despite the experience.

Some negative experiences are like manure, they help you to grow the real fruit. Some negative experiences are like stepping stones, they help you to reach your destination. If you can use the six-phase-scheme, you can conquer and tame any negative experience.

# ABOUT THE AUTHOR

Charles Mwewa (LLB. BA. Edu. + Engl., BA. Legal Studies. Cert. Law. DIBM. LLM.) is a Dad, author, and poet. Mwewa is the author of over 50 books and counting in all genres – fiction (novels), non-fiction and poetry. Mwewa, his wife, and their three girls, reside in the Capital City of Ottawa, Canada

Websites:
charlesmwewa.com
acpress.ca

Facebook:
facebook.com/authorcharlesmwewa

Email:
info@acpress.ca

Amazon:
amazon.com/dp/198825146X

# INDEX

## F

factors, 24
failures, 11
faith, 2, 9
fatigue, vii
favor, 2
feelings, 2, 17, 21, 26
forgiveness, 16
friends, 22
frustrating, 11

## G

goal, 13, 26
good news, 3
guilty, 15

## H

habit, 2, 5
history, 27
honey, 10
hope, 9
housewife, 7
humiliating, 11, 27
humiliation, 16, 19

## I

ideas, 1, 24
ignore, 11, 13, 16, 17
insulted, 11
isolation, 19

## J

job, 26
joy, 9

## L

legacy, 6
lethal, 14
liable, 15
love, 2, 9, 28
lowliness, 26

## M

major depressive disorder, vii
manifest, 27
marital breakdown, 26
medical terms, vii
medicine, 13
meditation, 1, 2
mental or emotional pressure,
    vii
messaging, 3
mind, viii, 1, 3, 5, 7, 13, 18
money, 9, 10
moods, 1, 5, 11
morning, 1, 2, 3
motivation, 20

## N

normalcy, 20